THE MINIATURE BOOK OF
Napkin Folding

a Salamander book

Published by Salamander Books Limited
LONDON • NEW YORK

Published by Salamander Books Ltd., 129-137 York Way,
London N7 9LG, United Kingdom.

© Salamander Books Ltd., 1990

Printed and bound in Belgium

ISBN 0 86101 550 9

CREDITS

PROJECTS BY: *Karen Lansdown and Susy Smith*

EDITED BY: *Jilly Glassborow*

PHOTOGRAPHY BY: *Steve Tanner*

DESIGN AND ARTWORK BY: *Pauline Bayne*

TYPESET BY: *SX Composing Ltd.*

COLOUR SEPARATION BY: *Chroma Graphics (Overseas) Pte. Ltd.*

Printed in Belgium by PROOST N.V.

Contents

Butterfly Napkin

ADD THE FINISHING TOUCH
TO EACH SETTING WITH
THIS CLASSIC FOLD

1 A crisply starched napkin is required for this design. Lay the napkin flat. Fold two edges to meet in the centre as shown. Then fold the half nearest you across the centre line and over on the top of the other half, to form a long, thin rectangle.

2 Fold the right-hand end of the rectangle in towards the centre, and with another fold double it back on itself as shown. Repeat with the left-hand side so that the double folds meet in the centre.

3 Pull the right-hand back corner across to the left, bringing the front edge across the centre line to form a triangle. Anchoring the right-hand side of the triangle with one hand, use the other hand to fold the corner back to its original position, thus creating the 'wings' of the arrangement. Repeat the process on the left-hand side.

Pure and Simple

THIS ELEGANT DESIGN IS
IDEAL WHEN FOLDING
LOTS OF NAPKINS

1 First fold the napkin in half diagonally, then bring the left- and right-hand corners up to meet at the apex.

2 Carefully turn the napkin over, flopping it from left to right, and fold the corner closest to you up slightly as shown.

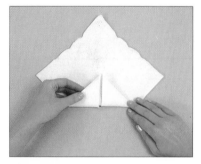

3 Fold the left- and right-hand corners underneath the napkin on a slight diagonal, pressing the folds lightly in place with your fingers.

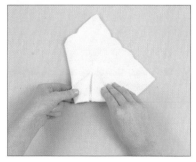

Pure Elegance

IDEAL FOR LARGE NUMBERS,
THIS POPULAR FOLD IS
FAST AND EASY

1 For best results use a crisply starched napkin to make this attractive fold. First fold the napkin lengthwise into three to form a long rectangle. Lay it horizontally with the free edge away from you, and fold the left- and right-hand ends in to meet in the centre.

2 Fold down the top right- and left-hand corners to meet in the centre, forming a point. Take the napkin in both hands and flip it over towards you so that the point is facing you and the flat side of the napkin is uppermost.

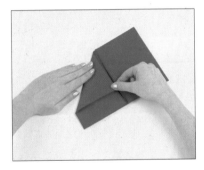

3 Lift the sides and pull them over towards one another to form a cone shape. Tuck the left-hand corner into the right-hand corner to secure it. Turn the napkin around and place it on a plate as shown opposite.

Double Jabot

THIS COMPLEX FOLD ADDS A
TOUCH OF ELEGANCE TO
ANY DINNER PARTY

1 Fold the napkin twice to form a square and position it with the loose corners at the top right. Fold the top corner back diagonally to meet the lower left corner, then turn it back on itself as shown. Continue to fold the corner back and forth to create a 'concertina' effect along the diagonal strip of napkin.

2 Lift the next layer of fabric from the top right-hand corner and repeat the process described above to create two parallel strips with zig-zag edges.

3 Pick the napkin up in both hands with the zig-zag folds in the centre. Fold it in half diagonally to form a triangle, keeping the pleats on the outside. Take the right-hand and left-hand corners of the triangle and curl them back, tucking one into the other to secure them. Stand the napkin upright on a plate as shown.

Lady's Slipper

THIS PRETTY AND SIMPLE
DESIGN IS IDEAL FOR
TEATIME SETTINGS

16

1 Begin by folding the napkin into four – left to right, top to bottom – to form a small square. Then fold the four loose corners back across the diagonal to form a triangle.

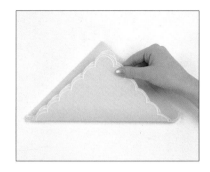

2 Holding the napkin firmly at the apex, fold one of the outer corners over and towards you as shown, so that it overlaps the base of the triangle. Repeat with the second corner so that the edges of both flaps meet down the centre of the napkin.

3 Turn the napkin over and fold the protruding flaps back over the base of the triangle. Then fold the triangle in half by pulling one of the corners over to meet the other. Finally, holding both corners firmly together, turn the napkin upright and pull the four loose corners upwards as shown in the main picture.

Lotus Blossom

THIS ATTRACTIVE FOLD IS
BASED ON A POPULAR
ORIGAMI DESIGN

1 The technique for this design is similar to that used in folding the origami 'fortune tellers' so popular with children. Using a well-starched napkin, lay the napkin flat, and begin by folding each of the four corners into the centre.

2 Repeat this same procedure, drawing the corners inwards to make an even smaller square. Then turn the napkin over and repeat for a third time, holding the corners down in the centre to keep them in place.

3 Still keeping your finger on the centre, reach behind the napkin to one of the corners tucked underneath, and draw this gently outwards as shown until it peaks out beyond the corner of the square. Repeat the process with all four flaps to form the petals. Finally, reaching underneath again, pull out the four single flaps to make the sepals.

The Bishop's Hat

DISPLAY THIS POPULAR FOLD
ON A FLAT SURFACE OR
IN A BOWL

1 Begin by folding the napkin diagonally to form a triangle, then pull each corner up to the apex as shown to form a square.

2 Turn the napkin over so that the free edges lie towards you. Pull the two top flaps up and away from you; then fold the remaining two flaps back in the same way to form a triangle.

3 Carefully turn the napkin over once more and pull the two outer corners together so that they overlap; tuck one flap into the folds of the other to hold them in place. Finally, turn the front of the 'hat' to face you, position the napkin upright and pull the loose flaps down as shown in the main picture.

Oriental Fan

GRACE YOUR DINNER TABLE
WITH THIS CHARMING,
EASY-TO-MAKE FOLD

1 This highly effective design benefits from a well-starched napkin. Begin by folding the napkin in half lengthwise and then fold one end of the oblong backwards and forwards in concertina-style folds, until just past the halfway point.

2 Holding the folds firmly together, fold the napkin lengthwise down the middle to bring both ends of the 'concertina' together. Keeping the folds in position in one hand, fold the loose flap of the napkin over across the diagonal.

3 Push the flap underneath the support as shown to balance the napkin, and, letting go of the pleats, allow the fan to fall into position.

Pocket Napkin

EMBELLISH THIS EASY FOLD
WITH A FEW FLOWERS
IN THE POCKET

1 Fold the napkin in half and then in half again to form a square; then fold it across the diagonal to form a triangle.

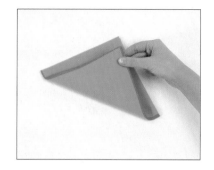

2 Position the napkin as shown with the four loose corners uppermost. Working with the top layer only, fold it down several times to make a cuff at the bottom.

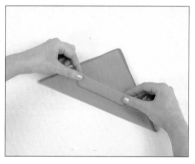

3 Fold the next (single) corner over so that the tip touches the top edge of the cuff. Fold the next two corners over to form three tiers. Finally, turn the right and left corners of the triangle to the underside and overlap them. Position the napkin as shown in the main picture and insert the flowers.

Four Feathers

THIS SIMPLE FOLD LOOKS
ELEGANT PLACED IN A
TALL WINE GLASS

1 Open the napkin flat. Fold it in half diagonally to form a triangle, and place the folded edge towards you. Place your index finger on the centre of this edge. Using the top layer of fabric only, bring the apex down to meet the left-hand corner.

2 Again working with the top layer only, bring the far corner down and across to the bottom left-hand corner.

3 Bring the remaining top corner down and across to the lower left corner as before, forming a triangle once more. Splay the folds slightly, then turn the napkin over so that the folds are underneath. Lift the edge and roll the napkin into a loose cone shape as shown, stopping about halfway across. Fold up the bottom point and insert the napkin into the glass.

The Princess

A BEAUTIFUL DESIGN SUCH
AS THIS REQUIRES SOME
TIME TO PERFECT

1 Fold the napkin in half to form a crease along the centre line. Then open the napkin out again. Fold one half of the napkin lengthwise into three by bringing the top edge of the square inwards to the centre line and then folding it back on itself as shown. Repeat with the second half.

2 Fold the napkin in half lengthwise by tucking one half under the other along the centre line. Lay the resulting strip flat with the three folded edges facing you. Mark the centre of this strip with a finger and fold the right-hand edge in towards the centre and back on itself as shown. Repeat with the left-hand side.

3 Pull the top left-hand corner across towards the top right-hand corner to create a triangle, pressing down gently along the folds to hold them in place. Repeat with the remaining left-hand folds, and then do the same with all the right-hand folds. Ease the folds open slighly and display the napkin with the centre point facing the guest.

Circular Napkin

EMBELLISH THIS CIRCULAR
FOLD WITH BEAD AND
RIBBON TRIMMING

1 Paint a plain 1in (2.5cm) wooden bead with a water-based paint to match your napkin. Then paint on a pattern with a harmonizing or contrasting colour. Allow the paint to dry between coats.

2 Fold the napkin in half once along its length, and then pleat it concertina-style along its length, making sure the folds are the same size.

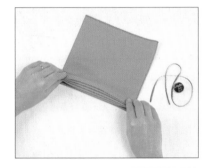

3 Thread a length of thin ribbon through the bead and tie it to hold the bead in place. Wrap the ribbon around the centre of the napkin, and tie it in a neat bow just below the bead. Fan the napkin out so that it forms a full circle.

Napkin Folder

HERE'S A QUICK AND EASY
WAY TO DRESS UP A
PLAIN NAPKIN

1 All you need for this pretty design is a square paper doily, preferably in a colour that contrasts with the napkin, and a floral motif. Begin by folding the napkin into a triangle.

2 Fold the doily diagonally. To create a 'spine' to allow for the thickness of the napkin, unfold the doily and make another crease about ⅜in (1cm) from the first fold.

3 Cut out a Victorian scrap or other floral motif and glue it to the centre of the smaller (top) side of the doily. Now simply insert the napkin.

Lacy Napkin Bow

FOR A WEDDING DINNER USE
THIS EASY-TO-MAKE LACY
NAPKIN BOW

1 Use a pretty napkin for this design, preferably with a lace detail around the edge. For each napkin you will need about 1yd (1m) of wide satin ribbon and the same amount of insertion lace.

2 For best results, the napkin should be starched and well ironed and folded into quarters. To cut decorative points for the ribbons and lace, fold the ends as shown and cut them diagonally.

3 Fold under two corners of the napkin to overlap in the centre, forming the shape shown here. Iron the folds flat. Lay the ribbon and lace flat, wrong side up, with the ribbon on top. Place the napkin on top and tie the ribbon and lace around it in a bow.

Net Napkin Ring

FOR A TOUCH OF FRIVOLITY
TIE TABLE NAPKINS IN
SHADES OF NET

1 For each napkin cut three different coloured rectangles of net, 18 by 13in (45 by 35cm). Fold each piece crosswise into three equal sections.

2 Fold the napkin twice to form a square, and then fold it diagonally to form a triangle. Now roll it lengthwise.

3 Place the lengths of net on top of each other, then tie them around the napkin. To finish, fan out the ends of the net as shown in the main photograph.

Floral Napkin

FOR A BREATH OF SUMMER,
TRIM A NAPKIN RING
WITH FLOWERS

1 Make the ring with artificial flowers so you can use it time and again, then finish off with a real flower. First, bend a short length of florist's wire into a circle and twist the ends together to secure them.

2 Wind some fine fuse wire around one or two small silk flowers – chosen to co-ordinate with your china and table linen. Then twist the ends of the fuse wire around the circle of florist's wire to hold the flowers in place.

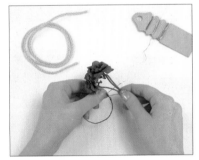

3 For covering the ring choose a fine ribbon or decorative braid. Hold one end in place with one hand, and use the other hand to twist the braid around the circle to cover it completely, beginning and ending underneath the flowers. Secure the ends with glue. Insert the napkin and add a fresh flower for the finishing touch.

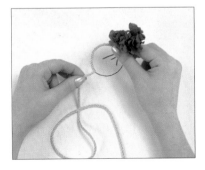

Tassel Napkin Ring

THIS GOLD TASSELLED NAPKIN
RING IS IDEAL FOR A
SPECIAL OCCASION

1 You will need two tassels and approximately 16in (40cm) of cord per napkin, and a strong fabric glue. Attach the tassels to the cord by wrapping the loop around the cord and pulling the tassels through it.

2 Make the ring by feeding the cord through both loops of the tassels twice more. Make sure that the ring is large enough to slip easily over the napkin.

3 Using a strong glue, secure the ends of the cord at the back of the ring. Lay one end along the back and trim it. Having applied the glue to the inside of the ring as shown, wrap the remaining end around the cords, covering the trimmed end. Cut this remaining piece of cord on the inside of the ring and clamp it in position until it is dry.

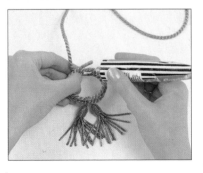

Thanksgiving

THE PERFECT SETTING FOR
A HARVEST FESTIVAL OR
THANKSGIVING MEAL

1 Use a sisal or straw placemat and a plain white napkin for this design. For the decoration you will need a selection of dried flowers and grasses and three lengths of beige or wheat-coloured ribbon, each about 20in (50cm) long.

2 Tie the lengths of ribbon together at one end. Plait them until the plait is long enough to tie around the napkin twice with a little left over.

3 Group the bunch of dried flowers and grasses together, securing them with thread or twine. Fold the napkin in half twice to form a long, thin rectangle. Lay the flowers on top of the napkin. Wind the plaited ribbon around the napkin and flowers twice and tie the ends under the napkin.

Stencilled Napkin

STENCIL YOUR OWN DESIGN
ON NAPKINS TO MATCH
YOUR CHINA

44

1 All you need for this design is a plain napkin or a hemmed square of fabric, a stencil motif – either bought or original, a natural sponge and some fabric paint.

2 Position the stencil on the napkin. Mix the paint in a saucer or palette. Dip the sponge into the paint and dab it on a piece of scrap paper to remove the excess. As an alternative to a sponge you can use a stencil brush, which will give a slightly different effect. It is worthwhile trying both to see which best suits your design.

3 You can either hold the stencil in place with your fingers or fasten it with tape. Dab paint through the stencil on to the fabric, taking care that it doesn't seep under the edges. When the paint is dry, fix it following the manufacturer's instructions.